Hello Everyone!

I am an elementary physical education teacher. I have been teaching for over 22 years and teach more than 250 students each day. Students come into class quiet and shy, new to school, and with many types of personalities. Getting to know some of these students individually and making a connection with them was becoming more and more challenging for me. As I struggled to develop teacher/student meaningful relationships, an idea hit me and it wouldn't leave my mind or heart. I went home after work one day and told my husband about an idea I had. I explained to him my struggles teaching at school and how I wanted to start some kind of an after-school group whose main purpose was to help me connect to more students, lift students' confidence and self-esteem, boost energy, and gain new friendships. He loved the idea!

I ran this idea by my principal the very next day and she didn't hesitate to give me the "Go For It"! I explained to her how I wanted to boost connections with my students, as well as help boost students' confidence, friendships, energy level, and self-esteem. I told her I didn't know what to name/call this club and she looked at me and said, "How about Booster Club?!" It was the perfect name for my group! Thank you Tina March for your encouragement and support for this idea! At that point, I began to make plans for our first 4th and 5th grade Booster (Boosting!) Club that year.

In the following pages there is a guide on how to run the club, an invitation letter to go home to parents/guardians, a letter of invitation to the student and 25 meeting plans ready to go to meet all the needs of your own Boosting Club. Call your club what you feel best fits your school. I call my club "Booster Club". If done efficiently, club meetings will take one hour. I chose every Tuesday after school for one hour starting in October. Each meeting is planned the same way to keep students from anxiety or fear. Have a blast!

My husband Mark has been the person who has encouraged me to write this book and I am so grateful for his editing help, support and love. I am also very grateful for my dad and mom, Larry and Nancy who helped me with editing and encouraged me throughout my journey. Thank you to my school friends who help to bring the best out of our students!

Who to invite?

I ask our 4th and 5th grade classroom teachers to submit to me names of students they feel could benefit from this after-school club. I give them from the first day of school until the end of September to get to know their students. By the end of September I ask the teachers to provide me with names of students who they feel need some boosting with friendships, socialization, confidence building, or self-esteem/energy raising.

How to invite?

I first send a letter home to the parent/guardian of these students. This letter is provided on the next page. Please feel free to use this one or create one that better suits your needs. This letter gives a brief outline of the club's purpose. It gives parents/guardians a chance to call and inquire and ask more questions about it or just sign it to give me permission to invite their child. Some parents don't sign it, so I don't invite their child. But for the parents who do sign it, I then proceed to give their child an invitation letter. This student invitation is also provided on the following pages. My goal is for the student to make the decision on their own if they want to attend or not. Once the student signs it, they are in! A club meeting date is set and now begins the amazing and incredible journey!

What happens during the one hour club time?

1. Meet at the same location once each week.
2. Check In: 10-15 minutes- As soon as everyone arrives have them sit in a circle either on the floor or in chairs. Ask the group a "Check-In" question and proceed around the circle asking

everyone to listen to each other's "Check In" answer by showing a respectful and caring attitude towards each other.

3. Walk and Talk: This is a time, about 15 minutes, when we learn and practice how to listen and carry on a conversation with others as they walk outside for a little exercise and social time. My rule for the Walk and Talk is they never walk alone or let others walk alone. This is a time where we get some exercise and we do it with others getting to know one another, sharing ideas and thoughts and just a time to talk about the school day they had. We never miss our Walk and Talk time. This is one of their favorite times. They enjoy going outside no matter how warm or cold it is and they love the fresh air, conversation, and energy it gives them.

4. Quick Snack Time (optional): I've done with and without snacks and it works great either way. If we do work snack time in, then it's a quick small bag of animal crackers or a fruit snacks. Some students choose not to have a snack so I encourage them to bring one from home but they rarely do. I feel this works out perfectly and gives students a chance at decision making on their own.

5. Activity time: This is a 15 to 25 minute time frame where there is a different planned activity. Rarely do I ever need to extend the activity into the next week's club time. There are one or two activities that do take a little extra time, but are such fun activities that it's worth spending 2 clubs on.

6. Group Cheer: We end each club by coming together with our hands in the middle and I ask one member to come up with a cheer for us to all say to end our time together for that week. It's like what a team does before going back out to play. The

students have really come up with creative and fun one, two, or three word cheers before we depart for home.

"Avocados from Mexico"!

"Dogs are great"!

"Minecraft"!

"Pizza"!

"Booster Club Is Great"!

4th and 5th Grade Teachers,

My goal is to start our afterschool Booster Club on Tuesday, Oct. 17th. I am looking for students to invite who may need a boost in meaningful friendships, a boost in confidence, they may seem shy or quiet, or they may need socialization practice, self-esteem enhancing, and or energy boosting. I will take your recommendations and first, send a letter home to parents explaining about our club and then with their permission, I will send a "letter of invitation" to the student. Please begin sending me names of students you feel may benefit from this opportunity.

Thank you for your time….Amy

Dear Parent or Guardian,

Several selected 4th and 5th grade students will soon be given the opportunity to be part of an exciting club at (your school).
This club is called the (name of club).   Its main purpose will be to lift students' confidence, self-esteem, energy, and gain new friendships. The purpose of this letter is to invite your son or daughter to be a member of our club.

This (club name) will meet every (day of the week) after school from (give the time it starts and time it ends) each week school is in session. For a full hour, students will be provided fun, energizing, and instructive activities free of charge. Involved students will be given a chance to interact, learn, and have fun with one another.

If you feel your son/daughter would benefit from the (name of the club) and would allow me to send them a personal invitation, please let me know by (date you want this returned). All that is required is for you to sign this letter below and a personal invitation will be extended to your son or daughter at school. It will then be their decision whether they would like to be a part of our after-school club. We will begin our (name of club) meetings on (club start date).

I will be personally overseeing club activities and welcome all ideas and questions. Thank you in advance for allowing our staff to work with your son or daughter in this unique and uplifting extension of the (school name) educational program.

(Name of club leader/teacher, school telephone number and email address)

Parent/Guardian Signature _____

Daughter/Son Name _____

Dear (first name of student),

I would like to invite you to be part of an exciting club at (school name). This club is called the (name of the school club).

The (club name) will meet every (day of week) after school from (time) each week school is in session. For a full hour, you will be provided fun, energizing, and instructive activities. You will be interacting, learning, and having fun with other students in the 4th and 5th grades.

If this would be something you would enjoy, please bring this letter to me signed by you and your parent or guardian. We will begin on (start date)!
Hope to see you there!

Your Friend,
(Club leader name)

Parent/Guardian Signature _____

Daughter/Son Signature _____

Parent/Guardian Telephone Number _____

Plunge Into Something New!

Club Meeting #1

Emphasis of the day

This first meeting is to provide the club members an opportunity to experience how the club will be run, to meet each other and have fun.

Check-In Question: Please tell us your name, what grade you are in, and what is your favorite thing to do?

Walk and Talk: Give everyone a chance to get coats on if needed and meet at the same door. Count the number of participants before going outside for your walk and talk. When everyone is there, remind students to find others to walk, talk, and listen to while walking together. Nobody is allowed to get out ahead too far and I always need to be able to see everyone and be able to give directions as to where we're walking and when we're done.

Snack Time: This is a short 5 minute time when students can get a small snack and sit down at a table with others to eat their snack. Allow about 5 to 6 minutes for eating and talking and then move on to the final group activity.

Group Activity Time: "Together Create" (Wenc, 1986)
Create A Masterpiece

Divide the club into groups of 3 or 4. Have them decide on an order of turns within their group. Each team can line up in front of a larger piece of white construction paper or poster paper taped to a wall or board or it can lay in the middle of a table. Let students choose whatever color of marker they wish to use when it's their turn up. The object of the game is for each group to create a picture together by taking turns, but they are only able to use a circle, or square, or triangle or 4 straight lines when it is their turn. During each turn they must add to the drawing. Remind the group that this isn't a race, but group artwork. Go until they seem to be out of ideas or until their group feels they are done. Share their work of art with the others. If time, repeat this activity.

Group Cheer: Don't forget this! It becomes a fun way to end each club time and gives various students an opportunity to come up with their own cheer for everyone to say together. It's fun and sometimes silly, but it helps us leave on a very happy and uplifting note.

"We Can" Extreme!

Club Meeting #2

Emphasis of the day

Continue to get to know one another, feeling more comfortable in our group, socializing, and working together.

Check-In Question: Tell everyone your favorite animal and why.

Walk and Talk: Before going on your walk & talk, discuss a little bit about what are some things you can talk about with your friends. Have the members come up with ideas on what to ask or how to start a conversation with members you know and with members you don't know.

Snack Time (optional): This is a short 5-minute time where students can get a small snack and sit down at a table with others to eat their snack. Allow about 5 to 6 minutes for eating and talking and then move on to the final group activity.

Group Activity Time: "Joint effort" (Wenc, 1986) Line Groups

Note: Try this at first letting them talk and if you feel they are ready for a challenge, have them try some without talking!

Divide group into groups of 5, 6 or 7, or divide the members into two groups, or however you want.

Have the smaller groups space out around the room.

Challenge #1 as a group: Make your line as long as you can.

Challenge #2 as a group: Make your line as short as possible.

Challenge #3 as a group: Without speaking, make your line with the shortest person in the front and the tallest person in the back.

Challenge #4 as a group: Line up according to your birthday, January to December. This can be done with or without speaking. Look at your time, and if you have some time to spare, have them try it without speaking.

Challenge #5 as a group: Line up in alphabetical order according to the first letter of your first name.

Challenge #6 as a group: Line up according to your birthday day.

2nd, 8th, 12th, 17th, 24th, 30th etc...

Challenge #7 as a group: Line up according to how many people are in your family.

Challenge #8 as a group: Line up by your shoe size. Smallest to Largest.

Group Cheer!! Don't forget this!

It's becomes a fun way to end each club time and it gives various students an opportunity to come up with their own cheer for everyone to say together. It's fun and sometimes silly, but it helps us leave on a very happy and uplifting note.

Distinctly You

Club Meeting #3

Emphasis of the day

Work on being more confident when speaking in front of others and practicing respectful listening skills.

Check-In Question: What are you excited about or looking forward to this week or weekend?

Walk and Talk: Before going on your walk & talk, remind students of possible topics to talk about, how to ask questions, listen, and how to respond to each other. Also remind everyone of the safety rules and nobody walks alone!

Snack Time (optional): This is a short 5-minute time where students can get a small snack and sit down at a table with others to eat their snack. Allow about 5 to 6 minutes for eating and talking and then move on to the final group activity.

Group Activity Time: "Get to know YOU"

Give everyone a 3x5 blank card and something to write with. Colored pencils is always fun.

Tell everyone you are going to ask them 5 questions and you would like them to write their answers down on the card so nobody can see. Please no talking during this time unless you have a question for me. When we are finished answering these questions, we will share our answers one at a time with everyone else. This activity is to help us get to know each other more deeply as a friend. I have the students stand up and either come to the front of the room or stand up at their chair.

1. What is your favorite bug and why?
2. What is your favorite holiday?
3. If you could be a Super Hero, what SUPER POWER would you want and why?
4. What do you think you would like to do when you grow up?
5. What quality do you think makes a good friend?

Group Cheer!! Don't forget this! Pick someone who hasn't had a chance yet and you feel really wants to.

Activation Collaboration

Club Meeting #4

Emphasis of the day

To be brave and get to know someone new in the group. To work as a group to practice social skills, collaborate and cooperate to complete a challenging task.

Check-In Question: If you could color your day a certain color, what color would you color it and why?

Walk and Talk: Challenge the group to walk with someone they don't know as well today.

Snack Time (optional): This is a short 5-minute time where students can get a small snack and sit down at a table with others to eat their snack. Allow about 5 to 6 minutes for eating and talking and then move on to the final group activity.

Group Activity Time: "Quick Look" (Jones, 1998)

You will need some kind of building blocks like Legos®, blocks, K'Nex®, etc…

Before the meeting, you will also need to make 2 or 3 small sculptures or designs. Hide them from the group. Make easier ones for lower functioning groups and more complex ones for higher functioning groups. Divide the group into small groups of 2-4 members. Give each group/team enough building material so that they can duplicate what you have already created. Place the original sculpture in a place that is hidden, but a close distance to all the groups. I put a tri-fold desk cardboard wall on a table and put my creation inside that. Ask the group to number themselves in order 1-2-3-4-etc...Ask #1 from each group to come at the same time to look at the sculpture for 5 seconds and try to remember it as much as possible before returning to his/her team.

After they get back to their teams, students have twenty-five seconds to instruct their teams how to build the structure so that it looks like the one that has been hidden. After the 25 seconds is over, ask the #2 member from each team to take a "Quick Look" for 5 seconds and then when the time is up, have them quickly go back to their group and add on to what has been done for twenty-five seconds. Continue to do this until you feel they are getting to a point where they are done. Show the groups the sculpture you made and let them see how close they were to the original masterpiece. Have each group showcase their sculpture to the group. It's so much fun and it's so good for them to communicate to others in a unique way.

Play again if there is time!!

Group Cheer!! Don't forget this!
Let them be creative and positive and even silly with the words they decide to say in the huddle. It is such a fun way to end the club meeting!!

Splendiferous Fun!

Club Meeting #5

Emphasis of the day

How to have fun even when there is competition. Show encouragement, kindness and patience.

Check-In Question: When is your birthday and share what you like or don't like about it.

Walk and Talk: Before going on a walk, talk about some conversation ideas they can have with their friends.

Snack Time: (optional)

Group Activity Time: "Pictionary-Group style"

Use small whiteboards or scratch paper, dry erase markers, eraser (if needed), pencils, and some kind of timer.

Randomly put members into groups of 3 and, if needed, a group of 4. Have each group come up with their team name! They love this and it helps them learn how to give and take and listen to other ideas.   Have simple words or pictures of simple objects ready for this game. I will go to our reading teacher in the building or kindergarten teachers and ask them for picture cards to use for this game. You can also use this site to find Pictionary words: (www.thegamegal.com) click on "word generator". There are easy, medium, hard, and medium-hard words as well as topics. I then ask the group to number off 1, 2, and 3 and to remember this order. The directions are for one person from each group to come to me to look at the object to draw without the guessers looking at the object. They return to their group to get ready to draw. No talking by the drawer! On the word GO, I start the timer for one minute or 30 seconds or whatever you think works best. The drawer begins drawing the object, trying to get the other players on his/her team to guess what he's drawing. The guessers have to be kind of quiet as they blurt out words so as not to give clues away to other groups. When they guess what the object is, the leader raises their arm and I watch to see which group answers first. I give a point to the team that guesses first. Sometimes there is a tie and I give a point to each group. I post the team names and write points under their name when their team earns a point. Now, it's number 2's turn to come up to get the next word/object to draw from each team. They go back get and ready, and on GO, they begin drawing while the others in the group try to guess what they are drawing. This game continues with lots of excitement and with about 3 minutes remaining we stop to add up points and <u>congratulate</u> each other.

Group Cheer!! Fun way to end! Pick someone who hasn't come up with a group/huddle ending. Brings hands together and on "3" we say whatever they chose. Make sure it's kind, respectful, and fun!

Heyro!

Club Meeting #6

Emphasis of the day

A time to get to know each other even more deeply. Accepting choices others make. Being brave to make your choice and to speak in front of others.

Check-In Question: Announcement: For the next Club Meeting, bring a fun joke to share for our check-in time. If someone is absent from the group, remind the members to tell those who aren't here today about our check-in for next time.

 If you were asked to give advice to someone, what advice would it be?

Walk and Talk: Remind everyone to make sure each club member is walking with someone, don't be the one who is always talking, be a good listener too, and ask questions.

Snack Time (optional): If you take time for a snack, don't let it last too long (4-5 minutes) and make sure everyone is sitting with others. Don't let anyone sit alone during snack time.

Group Activity Time: "4-Corners"

Tape a number 1, a number 2, a number 3 and a number 4 to four different corners or areas in the room. Tell students that they are to choose an answer to each upcoming question, note the associated number, and go to the corner labeled with that number. I only read one question at a time. It helps to write out in larger lettering on a piece of paper the four choices with the corresponding numbers for each question. This way they aren't asking what number goes with what choice. After each person has chosen a corner/area, ask them to choose a presenter and ask the members of each group to answer why they chose this group, or the advantages or disadvantages of the choice they made.

Question number 1: What kind of person do you consider yourself?
1- Dog Person
2- Cat Person
3- Dog & Cat Person
4- Not a cat or dog person

Question number 2: In your family, are you the…?
1- Oldest child
2- Youngest child
3- Middle child
4- Only child

Question number 3: What is your favorite season?
1- Spring
2- Summer
3- Winter
4- Fall

Question number 4: Choose one of these colors you like the best. You as a leader can use whatever colors you want.
1. Blues
2- Reds
3- Yellows
4- Greens

Question number 5: What do you enjoy doing in your spare time? You can change these to whatever you want. Some others options you could use are video games, cook, play with pets, watch television, play on the computer etc.

1- Board games

2- Play outside

3- Listen to music or read a book

4- Play with friends

Question number 6: What is your favorite kind of ice-cream?

    1- Chocolate

    2- Vanilla

    3- Cookie Dough

    4- Other kind

Question number 7: Where would you like to go on vacation or visit? (You can change these to whatever you want).

1- Amusement Park

2- Campground

3- Ocean

4- Mountains

Group Cheer!! Don't forget-this is a very important way to end the time with the group!

Tower Power!

Club Meeting # 7

Emphasis of the day

Practice telling a joke. Group challenge, problem solve and work positively with others.

Check-In Question: Share a joke with everyone. Here are some suggestions for the leaders.

1. What do you call people who carry a calculator in their pants pocket?- Smarty Pants
2. Where does Frosty the Snowman keep his money?- In a Snow bank
3. Why did Dracula join the baseball team?- He wanted to be the bat boy
4. What is a hog's favorite sport?- Pig Pong
5. Which dog always knows what time it is?- A watch dog
6. What fish goes well with peanut butter in your sandwich?-A jelly fish
7. What has 18 legs and catches flies?- A baseball team
8. What animal runs around the classroom stealing answers?-A cheetah
9. What's a snake's favorite subject?- Hiss-tory
10. What are the largest ants in the world?- Gi-ants

Walk and Talk: Remind everyone to make sure each club member is walking with someone. Don't be the one who is always talking, but be a good listener too, and ask questions.

Snack Time (optional): If you take time for a snack, don't let it last too long (4-5 minutes) and make sure they pick up after themselves. I constantly remind my members of the importance of leaving our space the same way we found it and, if we can, even better!

Group Activity Time: "Paper Skyscraper" (Jones, 1998)
Paper Tower

Put members in groups of 3, no more than 4, and no less than 2. Find a stack of scrap 8 ½"X 11" papers if you can. (Copy machine kind is best).

Give the group a stack of paper to start with and give them the challenge to see how tall they can build a tower with their paper. All they are allowed to use is their paper, brains, and hands. You can limit them to 10-15 sheets of paper or use whatever amount they want!

You can give them a goal to try to build a tower 5 sheets high. There are many ways to fold and build the tower. Let them be creative and see if they can use each other's ideas to build the tallest paper building!

Take pictures! The students love to pose and they get so excited! Give them a picture to take home if you want.

Group Cheer!! Make sure the students help pick up the paper and find a recycle container for the used pieces.

Give someone new a chance to come up with your huddle cheer. Or, you the leader can come up with one this time.

Rope Cowabunga

Club Meeting # 8

Emphasis of the day

Learning to encourage, listen to one another, and team cooperation.

Check-In Question: Share one thing you are grateful for.

Walk and Talk: We walk outside no matter what the temperature, but if it is extremely cold and windy or raining, we will either walk the halls for a while or walk laps in the gym. I like keeping the same routine for the members so they know what to expect for each meeting. I do shorten or lengthen the walks a little bit depending on the type of day it is or the type of activity I have planned!

Snack Time (optional): Don't let anyone sit alone during snack time. I don't provide drinks, just a simple snack if they want. A few students opt out of the snack, but that's ok and their choice. If students would like a drink of water, I give them time to get a quick drink during this time.

Group Activity Time: My meetings have been in various rooms in the school. I have had meetings in classrooms, art rooms, gyms, and the library. I like our library because it has tables and is a larger area than the classrooms, but not too big like the gym.

"Rope Togetherness" (Wenc, 1986) Cooperative Strings

For this activity, I ask to use the gym for this fun cooperation game. After our snack, we move to the gym. Depending on the size of

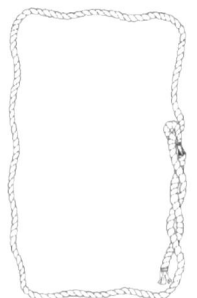

your group, I divide the members into two groups of 7 or 8. If you have enough students to work with, I think it's better to have two separate groups but if all you have is 7, 8, or 9 members do it all together. I have ready to go 2 very long ropes of at least 20 feet or more to make it more challenging or you can use much shorter ropes and the members will be standing more closely together. I have the ends of each rope tied together. Each person holds the rope with both hands and makes a circle where they are standing holding the rope on the outside of the circle. Each group has their own area in the gym. The object of the game is to see how fast each group can work together without letting go of the rope and keeping both hands on the rope to make the shapes I give them. Sometimes I have to put a time limit on how long they have, 2 minutes, or 1 ½ minutes, etc... or you can spice it up even more and give them one where they can't talk!

Here are the various shapes;

1. Oval
2. Square
3. Triangle
4. Mountains
5. Diamond (kite)
6. Rectangle
7. Star
8. Half-Circle
9. Canoe shape
10. School building

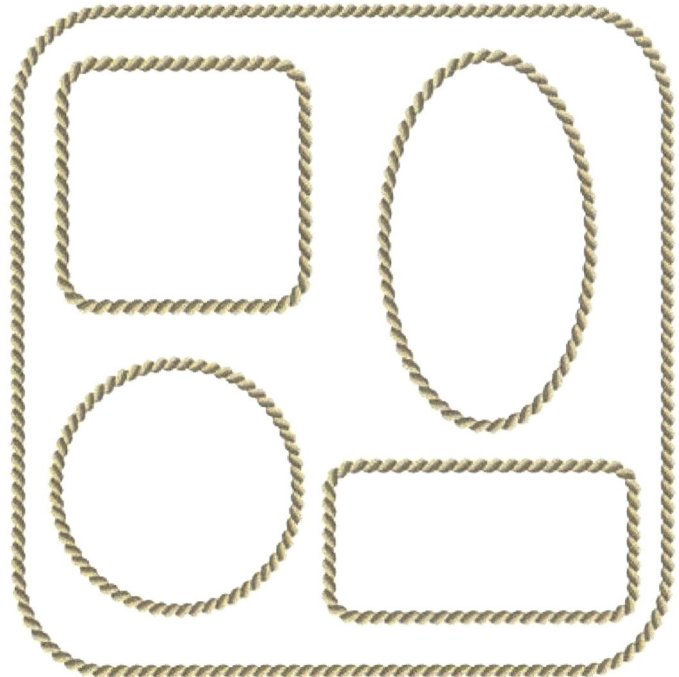

Group Cheer!! Being a former athlete and coach of many sports, I enjoy the group huddle, too. On very rare occasions I decide on what to say for our huddle cheer before it's time to depart. Because I like to keep things simple I usually go with positive joyful and simple words that will boost the group.

Cheer Ideas:

"Together!"

"Booster Club!" (that's the name of OUR group)

"WE CAN!"

"Yay For The Day!"

…You get the gist….☺

A Lot Like Me

Club Meeting #9

Emphasis of the day

To learn the similarities between themselves and others, to be able to learn how to approach others, and learn how to ask a question of others.

Check-In Question: What is your favorite kind of cookie?

Walk and Talk: Remind the students of things they can talk about while on our walk.

Snack Time (optional): As a leader of the group, I usually take this time to organize my activity and get it ready. If I don't need a lot of time to do this, I will usually sit in with a group who are conversing while eating their snack. It gives me a great insight into their interests.

Group Activity Time: "Who Else?" (Wenc, 1986)

Have each member get the paper with the questions on it and a pencil. Tell them that they are to answer each question by interviewing the others in the group. They are to answer each item as closely as they with a group member's name.

Who else?...

1. has the same shoes on as you.
2. likes the same t.v. show as you.
3. likes the same subject in school as you.
4. lives the closest to your house.
5. has as many brothers and sisters as you.
6. likes the same sport as you.
7. likes the same kind of music as you.
8. has the same color eyes as you.

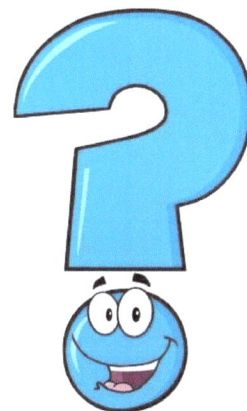

9. likes to do the same kind of thing as you do in your spare time.
10. likes the same color as you do.

Ask the group what they found out and what they learned about each other.

Group Cheer!! Don't forget this special ending!

Gettin' Goofy

Club Meeting # 10

Emphasis of the day

To learn how to get up in front of others and be a good sport. Understand and learn games are played to have fun with others.

Check-In Question: If you could eat lunch with anyone, who would he or she be?

Walk and Talk: As the weather changes, make sure everyone is wearing proper clothing for a walk outside. I've had members try to get away with not wearing a coat on a day a coat is needed to be worn. We don't want to have to shorten a walk and talk time just because of this.

Snack Time (optional): Continue to give ideas to the students of what they can talk about at a table. Explain what a table conversation looks like and sounds like. Remind them to pick up after themselves and not be sloppy.

Group Activity Time: "Charades"

The students love this activity. Charades can be played in many different ways. This is the way I like to play. It can be played throughout the year and it's also good to do if you have 10 or so extra minutes at the end.

Have a timer available. I put members into 2 groups, and then ask each group to give their team a name and number each individual in the group. (1-8…) I ask for player #1 from the first group to come up and pick a word out of a hat/cup. I go to the website www.thegamegal.com to generate words for me to use for this game. This is a great site to use for words and ideas. It also has printable words. There is a set of printable words that have Easy Words- Medium Words- Hard Words- and Really Hard words. I print these up, cut them out, and the students can pick a word from any of the 4 cups that I have marked as to what type of word it is, Easy, Medium, Hard, or Really Hard. This site can also generate season or holiday words which I have used as well as many others. I use this site for my Charades Games as well as my Pictionary game activity. I give them about 10 seconds to think about how they are going to get their team to guess the word. I set about 30 seconds or a little less (you decide) and I say GO! Without talking or pointing to anything or anyone, one member from one team tries to get their team to guess the word. If they guess it, I give a point to that team, and now the other team's #1 gets to try, and so on. We continue this game giving everyone a chance to do a charade until the end of our club time. They love it and have a lot of fun playing it!

Group Cheer!!

Group Cheer!! I try to check with a student before we start our meeting or sometime during the actual school day to see if they would be interested in coming up with our group cheer at the end of our club time. They feel it is a privilege and an honor to be the one chosen to do this. This is an important part of ending our group meeting. We all leave with a smile after our cheer.

Totally Talkin'

Club Meeting # 11

Emphasis of the day

Practice and learn how to talk to each other, ask questions, and listen to others.

Check-In Question: If you could change one rule that your family has, what would you change?

Walk and Talk: Remind everyone to make sure each club member is walking with someone, don't be the one who is always talking, be a good listener too, and ask questions.

Snack Time (optional): If you take time for a snack, don't let it last too long (4-5 minutes) and make sure everyone is sitting with others. Don't let anyone sit alone during snack time.

Group Activity Time: "The Dice Game"

You will need dice for this game (one for each person) and a small card with the following questions on it. You can play with just one set of questions or you can have two or three sets of questions so that various questions are asked. Either works great!

1. Tell me something you are good at.
2. What do you like about spring? (any season)
3. Tell me something about your family.
4. What is your favorite animal and why?
5. What is something you are proud of?
6. What do you like about school?

1. What is your favorite color and why?
2. What is your favorite holiday and why?
3. How do you feel right now and why?
4. What has been your favorite vacation and why?
5. Tell me a book you have read lately?
6. What kind of music do you like?

1. What is your favorite video game you like to play and why?
2. What is your favorite food?
3. What is your middle name? Does your name mean anything that you know of?
4. What is your favorite number and why?
5. What is your favorite sport or sport team?
6. What is your favorite subject in school and why?

Each person gets a card with six questions on it as well as a die. When the music starts, the group begins to walk around not touching others and in the same area. When the music stops, they have to find the closest person (preferably someone new) and stand in front of them. Each will roll a die when it is their turn and ask each other the question that corresponds with the number from their card. Example: When I find my new partner, I roll my die and they ask me a question from their card that corresponds with the number on their card. After I'm finished with my answer, my partner rolls their die and I look at my card and ask them the question that corresponds with the number on my card.

Group Cheer!! Don't forget this important part of the club! With
about 2 minutes left in the time, I stop the activity and ask the students to pick up and clean up better than it was before we got there. Now it's time for your group huddle and cheer!

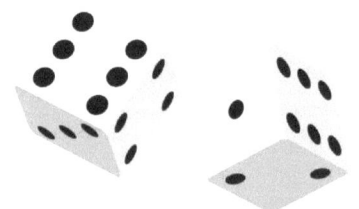

Friends Are "Fur"ever

Club Meeting # 12

Emphasis of the day

Learn to be respectful to guest speakers and how to treat guests properly who come to visit.

Check-In Question: How can you make your next day better?

Walk and Talk: Remind everyone to make sure everyone is walking with someone, don't be the one who is always talking, be a good listener too, and ask questions.

Snack Time (optional): There may be a rare occasion when you won't have time for a snack. If this is the case, please don't worry about it. The kids don't mind missing a snack and it's also good for them to practice change and/or managing emotions.

Group Activity Time: This may take a little time to set up, but it's well worth it for the students. I have done this two times in the 4 years of our club. I need to make sure to do it each year. I found someone from the community to bring a dog to our club. One year, I found grandparents of a student from the school who rescued a dog who had a bad leg. They adopted him and this dog now has a special foot they strap on to him for him to be able to walk. They take this special foot off each night while he sleeps. This same dog has also become a therapy dog and visits senior care centers, hospitals, schools, and libraries. The couple brought the dog to our club and explained about the life of the dog, how his leg became injured, and gave the

students time to pet the dog and ask questions. It was a wonderful and inspiring meeting.

The second time we had a dog visit our club, the dog came from our community Humane Society. An older gentleman brought an older and very gentle and kind dog to our club. He talked to the group about how to approach dogs and their owners, how to care for a dog, and the important responsibilities of owning a dog. He also gave any student who wanted the opportunity to pet him. It was another great guest speaker.

The next meeting I gave the students a few minutes to write thank-you notes to our guest speakers and I sent it to them through the mail. This, of course, is optional if you don't have time.

Group Cheer!! If you don't have time for a cheer today, no worries, having a dog visit is so much fun and well worth it.

Taking Off!

Club Meeting # 13

Emphasis of the day

Find enjoyment in competition and praising others.

Check-In Question: What is your favorite thing about school?

Walk and Talk: Remind everyone to make sure each club member has someone to walk with. Give suggestions of topics to talk about.

Snack Time (optional): If you take time for a snack, don't let it last too long (4-5 minutes) and make sure everyone is sitting with others. Don't let anyone sit alone during snack time.

Group Activity Time: I used to love making paper airplanes as a kid and took pride in how pointed I could get the tip. So one of the activities students really have enjoyed over the years is learning how to make "my" paper airplanes. I find a good stack of recycled 8 1/2 x 11 paper. Each student gets a few sheets and I teach them how to make a paper airplane. I go slow and make sure everyone keeps up with me. I also encourage each student to help one another. We continue until finished and some will want to make theirs their own way. I encourage that if there's time. We then go to the gym, though any large area would work great (even outdoors if there's no wind). We take turns either playing a short game of 5-hole or 6-hole paper-airplane golf. I put them in groups of 2 or 3 and they see how many shots it takes for them to land on or in each hula hoop. Students count and keep track of their shots.

You can also make it simpler if the group is smaller, (5-9). I put three different hoops out in front of the group. One is placed a short distance away, another a little farther, and the third one the farthest away. They take turns to see which hoop their airplane lands closest to and that's how many points they get. Closest to the shortest hoop (2 points), medium (5 points), farthest away (10 points). I give extra points if they land inside a hoop. Have them add up their points as they take their turns. I always encourage good sportsmanship, support, helpful hints to each other, and fair play and honesty.

Group Cheer!! Keep this fun and light-hearted. All the students should leave with smiles on their faces and maybe even giggling. You want them leaving excited for next week's meeting.

Sound & Seek

Club Meeting # 14

Emphasis of the day

Cooperation, enjoyment, fairness, discipline and learning to accept winning graciously or not winning politely.

Check-In Question: Share one accomplishment or talent you are proud of and why.

Walk and Talk: Very important part of the club time. I have found over the years this is one activity the kids LOVE!

Snack Time (optional): If you take time for a snack, don't let it last too long (4-5 minutes) and make sure everyone is sitting with others. Don't let anyone sit alone during snack time.

Group Activity Time: "Owl & Duck"

Divide the group into two teams. You need two unlike objects to be able to hide. One player is chosen from each team and is sent out of the room. While they are out of the room, one person from each team hides the other team's object. The two players return and begin to look for their own team's' object. Members of the teams "whoo, whoo" or "quack" according to the nearness their player is to their object. First player to find the object wins a point for the team. Choose new finders and hiders and play again.

The students are going to get louder and louder so you need to have a way to keep the noise level to a minimum. The players whooing or quacking are also going to want to move around. The rule is they stay seated. No talking or moving their arms or hands or heads. They are only allowed to use their sound to help their player find the object. I have used other noises besides "whoo" or "quack".

Group Cheer!! Don't forget this very important ending to the meeting. It's fun to hear the cheers students comes up with.

Better Than Words!

Club Meeting # 15

Emphasis of the day

Learn to always play fairly, honestly, and unselfishly.

Check-In Question: What is the hardest thing about your school day?

Walk and Talk: As a club leader, I enjoy the walk and talk too. I make sure though that I don't walk and talk with only one student. Sometimes I just walk alone and monitor everyone. Most times, I find a group of 2 or 3 students walking together and I join in with them. For some students, it's very easy to talk with an adult so I make it a rule to not walk and talk with just one student. I either walk alone or with a group of students.

Snack Time (optional): If you take time for a snack, don't let it last too long (4-5 minutes) and make sure everyone is sitting with others. Don't let anyone sit alone during snack time.

Group Activity Time: "Signs"

Start by sitting everyone in a circle facing inwards. I used chairs for this, but I'm sure you could sit on the floor. Each person should choose their own unique "sign", which is a movement or motion such as touching their nose, brushing their teeth, giving two thumbs up, etc. Go around the circle and give people the chance to demonstrate their sign to the rest of the group.

Choose someone to be the "GUESSER". Have the "GUESSER" close his/her eyes while you choose someone in the circle to start the action. The "GUESSER" can stand outside the circle and when you're ready you can tell the "GUESSER" to open his/her eyes. The person you choose to start the action has to secretly pass the sign onto another player without being caught by the "GUESSER". To pass, you must make YOUR sign followed by the sign of the player you are passing to.

The game continues until someone is caught by the "GUESSER", then you choose another new "GUESSER".

Group Cheer!! Depending on the size of your group, by now you are getting down to the last few people to give the opportunity to come up with a group cheer. If you have used everyone, then it's time to start over and give one or more students a second chance.

Columbus and Me!

Club Meeting # 16

Emphasis of the day

To learn, practice and participate in group decisions.

Check-In Question: Tell about something you collect or would like to collect.

Walk and Talk: Suggest several topics to talk about and remind everyone of the "Walk and Talk" expectations.

Snack Time (optional): Sometimes students will try to sit alone, but I never allow it. I make sure everyone is sitting with others.

Group Activity Time: "Your Country" (Jones, 1998) Create A Country

Depending on how many students you have, put groups together with two, three or no more than four people. You will need large pieces of white bulletin board paper (one for each group) and pens, pencils, colored markers, and colored pencils or crayons.

Give the groups the following story and then let them create!!

   "You and your crew mates have claimed an uninhabited island as a new country. You and your crew have been selected to be the new government in charge. Your mission is to make the following decisions and accomplish the following tasks, and then draw it all out on your large poster paper. Here is what your group needs to decide and draw on the paper.

Have these 7 tasks posted so all can see it and refer to it.

1. Draw an outline of your country
2. Name your country
3. Design your flag
4. Name and draw your National bird
5. Name and draw your National flower
6. Make 3 important laws for your country
7. Appoint each person a job serving the needs of the country.

The group must work together to complete the task and then have them present their country to the rest of the groups. This activity will take more than one club meeting. I have used 2 or 3 clubs to finish and present. This is one of their favorite activities. A lot of creativity and teamwork happens.

Group Cheer!! Don't forget to do this last part. It helps everyone leave on a happy note!!

COOLio!!

Club Meeting # 17

Emphasis of the day

Being brave- to be able to stand and speak in front of a group to present their finished project.

Check-In Question: Share a manner you think is really important and you think should be followed everyday by everyone.

Walk and Talk: If there is ever a time because of a shortened walk, be prepared with a short, fun, and easy to organize activity to fill at the end.

Snack Time (optional): If you take time for a snack, don't let it last too long (4-5 minutes) and make sure everyone is sitting with others. Don't let anyone sit alone during snack time.

Group Activity Time: This will be the day you give each group about 5 minutes to finish up the drawing and organize the group presentation of "Your Country".

After each presentation, I will let the others in the club ask about 2 or 3 questions to the presenters. Every year the audience will praise and tell the presenters what they really liked about their country. This activity truly brings out the best in students! I will display all country creations somewhere in the school as long as I have the permission of every student in each group.

Group Cheer!! This only takes 1 minute to do so please don't forget it!

Fabulosity!

Club Meeting # 18

Emphasis of the day

To be proud of yourself and the unique qualities you possess. To be brave in letting others know about your uniqueness. To accept others distinctive qualities in a respectful way.

Check-In Question: What is something you would like to be better at?

Walk and Talk: Dress for the weather!

Snack Time (optional): If you take time for a snack, don't let it last too long (4-5 minutes) and make sure everyone is sitting with others. Don't let anyone sit alone during snack time.

Group Activity Time: "One of A Kind" (Jones, 1998)
Unique Qualities

Using 3x5 cards and pencils have each person write their name on the front of the card and have them write five unique qualities they like about themselves, trying to come up with qualities that others might not know about them. Have the students hand you all the cards and mix them up in your hands. Now read the cards and have the students write down who they think it is. Go through each card stating each quality and let everyone know who has the unique qualities. See which student guessed the most correctly. This is really a lot of fun and the students enjoy learning interesting qualities about others.

Group Cheer!! If YOU haven't done a cheer yet, this might be a great time to do it.

The Artistects

Club Meeting # 19

Emphasis of the day

Communication, teamwork, problem solving, leadership, flexibility and negotiation.

Check-In Question: Who do you admire the most and why?

Walk and Talk: Dress for the weather!

Snack Time (optional):

Group Activity Time: "Marshmallow Tower"

For this activity you will need packages of big marshmallows and small marshmallows and packets of spaghetti.

Put your students in groups of 3, 4, or 5. You don't want too many per group. I like 3 or 4 people per group.

The goal is to see which group builds the highest tower by using only the items provided. The towers must be stable.

An alternate way is to ask the groups to make a sculpture with limited items given to them. Either challenge/idea works great.

Give them as much possible time as possible and then, with about 7 minutes left, have each group walk around and look at the other groups' towers/sculptures. You can have each group present their tower/sculpture if you think that works best.

Group Cheer!! Make sure all students have had a chance to make up a cheer for the group!

School Pride

Club Meeting # 20

Emphasis of the day

To feel satisfaction in participating in a community service project.

Check-In Question: What is your favorite ice cream?

Snack Time (optional): If you take time for a snack, don't let it last too long (4-5 minutes) and make sure everyone is sitting with others. Don't let anyone sit alone during snack time.

Group Activity Time and Walk and Talk (do this together):

I pick a day in the spring when I know it's going to be fairly nice outside. I try to do this more towards the end of the school year with about 3 or 4 weeks left of our club meetings.

I ask our custodian for rubber gloves and about 6 plastic trash bags and have them ready for our club to use. I ask everyone to form groups of 2 or 3 or I do that for them. I hand out one bag to each group and ask them to take turns holding it for the group. I explain to the group that our activity for today is a community service project. Our community is our school. We take pride in this building and the surrounding area. I tell them that today we are going to clean up our school grounds. With rubber gloves on we are going to find litter outside on our school property and pick it up and throw it away! I tell them to NOT pick up glass. When finished, we throw the bags of trash away, go back inside the building to wash our hands, and then gather and talk about how it feels to volunteer? How do they feel after helping clean up our school.

The next day at school I will (or ask the principal to) thank the group for cleaning the school property. I have it announced over the school speaker during school announcements so the whole school hears.

Group Cheer!! Don't forget!!

Dare to Draw

Club Meeting #21

Emphasis of the day

Acceptance, emotion control, teamwork, fairness, and encouragement

Check-In Question: What is your favorite meal at home or what is your favorite school meal?

Walk and Talk: Dress for the weather!

Snack Time (optional): If you take time for a snack, don't let it last too long (4-5 minutes) and make sure everyone is sitting with others. Don't let anyone sit alone during snack time.

Group Activity Time: Pictionary-Group Style (We did this back in club #5). Use this site to find Pictionary words: www.thegamegal.com, click on "word generator". There are easy, medium, hard, and medium hard, as well as topics. I'm repeating this activity because the students really love this one. I think it brings out the best in them and has great value.

Use small whiteboards or scratch paper, dry erase markers, eraser if needed, pencils, and some kind of 1-minute timer.

Randomly put members into groups of 3, if needed, a group of 4. Have each group come up with their team name! They love to use their creativity and it helps them learn how to give and take and listen to other ideas. Have simple words or pictures of simple objects ready for this game. I will go to our reading teacher in the building or kindergarten teachers and ask them for picture cards to use for this game. I then ask the group to number off 1, 2, and 3 and to remember this order. The directions are for one person from each group to come to me to look at the object without the guessers looking at the object. They return to their group to get ready to draw. No talking by the drawer! On the word GO, I start the timer for one minute or 30 seconds, or whatever you think works best. The drawer begins drawing the object trying to get the other players on his/her team to guess what he/she is drawing. The guessers have to be fairly quiet as they blurt out words not to give clues away to other groups. When they guess what the object is, the leader raises their arm and I watch to see which group answers first. A point is given to the team that guesses first. Sometimes there is a tie so I give a point to each group. I post the point under their team name. Now, it's number 2's turn, and so on, to come up to get the next word/object to draw from each team. They go back to their team, and get ready, and on GO, they begin drawing while the others in the group try to guess what they are drawing. This game continues with lots of excitement! With about 3 minutes remaining, we stop to add up points and congratulate each other.

Group Cheer!! Keep this going! Kids love it!

Let's Fly A Kite!

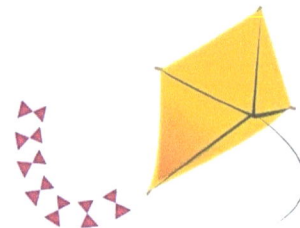

Club Meeting #22

Emphasis of the day

Outdoor enjoyment, persistence and helpfulness.

Check-In Question: What is your favorite team or music group?

Walk and Talk: Please don't forget this time. You can make it as short as you need in order to get the activity in. It is an important part of the club.

Snack Time (optional): If you want, you can have snack time be outside since the activity for today is outside or you can skip the snack altogether today.

Group Activity Time: "Fly a Kite"

For this activity, I go to a dollar store and pick up 10-15 cheap kites, enough so there is one kite for groups of two. We put the kites together like the directions say and then learn to fly them! Many students have never flown a kite, so I give pointers as to how to fly them best. This is such a fun activity and I get joy out of watching their faces and listening to their excitement as these simple kites fly in the air.

With about 5 minutes left, I ask them to gather their kites and wind up the string to be put away and we give a group cheer outside before we go.

Group Cheer!! Do this outside after the kites are gathered. I try to use my time efficiently because an hour goes very fast.

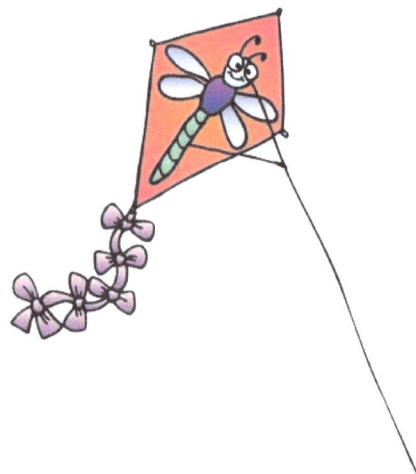

Rocktacular!

Club Meeting # 23

Emphasis of the day

Showing genuine friendship, kindness, and thoughtfulness.

Check-In Question: If I could travel anywhere in the world, where would it be?

Walk and Talk: Remind the group of expectations of this activity.

Snack Time (optional): If you take time for a snack, don't let it last too long (4-5 minutes) and make sure everyone is sitting with others. Don't let anyone sit alone during snack time.

Group Activity Time: "You Are Special"

Sit in a loosely formed circle either on the floor or in chairs at tables and give everyone a piece of paper and a pen or pencil or a couple of their favorite colored markers or pencils. Each person should write their name at the top of the piece of paper. When everyone is ready, have each student pass their paper to the person on their left. Each person then writes one (two, if you don't have a very large group) positive characteristics about the person who's name is at the top of the paper. After 30 seconds or so, everyone passes the pieces of paper to the left again and writes a positive characteristic about the next person whose name is at the top of that paper. Continue this passing until everyone has their own paper back.

Please walk around and make sure everyone is writing positive, encouraging, and thoughtful descriptive words. I usually have a list of a few words ready to help students if they're struggling with coming up with different and unique words. This is helpful to the student and it also moves the activity along. When everyone receives their piece of paper back again, the activity is over.

There are a couple of ways you can finish. You can collect all the papers and then hand them out one at a time, presenting each person with his or her paper and saying out loud some of the positive things that were written about them. Secondly, you can have students take time to read their own papers without sharing out loud.

This activity can be quite an amazing and gratifying activity for the students. Many students don't often get to hear or read nice things or kind words said about them from their peers. I encourage students to take these special papers home and post them where they can see and be reminded of their special traits.

Group Cheer!! Always end with an all-together cheer with all hands in the middle. It's a fun way to end club time!

Make 'Em Laugh

Club Meeting #24

Emphasis of the day

Cooperation, collaboration, flexibility, creativity, and listening skills.

Check-In Question: What is something you are looking forward to next year in 5th or 6th grade? Or ask… what was your favorite part of 4th or 5th grade?

Walk and Talk: Remind everyone to make sure each club member is walking with someone, don't be the one who is always talking, be a good listener too, and ask questions.

Snack Time (optional): Don't let anyone sit alone during snack time.

Group Activity Time: "Create a Cartoon"

This is a fun activity and will take a little preparation time. I found various simple 3 to 6 frame newspaper cartoons in the Sunday paper. I choose cartoons that are positive and happy and had at least 4-6 bubbles in them. I put whiteout over the words in the bubbles and then photocopied the cartoons. You can do this in black and white or in color, it really doesn't matter. I put students in groups of two and have them pick out a cartoon and take it back to their table area. The directions are to come up with words to put in the bubbles that match the facial expressions and the actions of what was going on in the frames. Students come up with their own words to go with the cartoons. When finished, if there is time, each student can pick a new one to do. When time is over, I have each student share their cartoons with the group by putting the cartoon under (what we have at our school) a Lady Bug (a document camera). Revised cartoons can be projected onto a screen for everyone to see and read! It is a lot of fun and the students are able to be creative.

Group Cheer!! Keep it simple and fun!

54

Finale Rally!

Club Meeting #25 Final Club of the school year!

Emphasis of the day

Learning to give your best to others and learning how to receive something with a grateful heart.

Check-In Question: Please share your favorite part of this club for this year.

Walk and Talk: Make it fun and enjoyable since this is the last club for the school year.

Snack Time: Whether you have done snacks this year or not I always end the last club with a special snack. I make homemade chocolate chip ice cream cookies every year for the group on the last day. They love them and are so grateful. Don't worry if you have one or two students who don't eat it. It's ok, that's their choice. You decide what treat you want to end with, it can be anything you feel is special and that your group will like.

Group Activity Time: "From Me To You" (Alanna Jones, 1996) Gift From The Heart

This is an amazing activity and a perfect way to finish. I assign everybody a partner. My direction to students is for each to find a spot in the room by themselves (not with their partner) with a piece of white construction paper and colors, markers, pencils, and pens that I've made available to use. Each person chooses an imaginary gift to give to their partner. Students are asked to draw and describe his or her gift on the piece of paper. I tell students they can be very creative with their gift and that they are to be thoughtful with their gift choice for their partner. This can be a drawing of something emotionally deep and creative, something their partner can use, or something imaginary but special for their partner.

Once everyone has finished their drawing, (about 10 min.) bring everyone together and have them sit with their partner. Please take time to let each person one at a time give their gift/drawing to his or her partner. Let others see it, hear what the gift is, and let the person receiving it show their gratitude. This is an amazing and delightful activity. It's such a special way to finish and each club member gets to take his or her gift/drawing home with them. It's wonderful!

Group Cheer!! You have to finish with a group cheer! However you wish to do it, always finish STRONG and HAPPY!!

References

Alanna Jones, C. (1996). *The Wrecking Yard of Games and Activities.* Ravensdal, WA: Idyll Arbor, Inc.

Jones, A. (1998). *104 Activities That Build.*

Wenc, C. C. (1986). Cooperation: Learning Through Laughter 2nd Edition. In C. C. Wenc, *Cooperation: Learning Through Laughter.* Minneapolis: Educational Media Corporation.

www.ingramcontent.com/pod-product-compliance
Lightning Source LLC
LaVergne TN
LVHW072107070426

835509LV00002B/53